# Facing Addiction

Three
True
Stories

## Beth Johnson

 **THE TOWNSEND LIBRARY**

# Facing Addiction:
# Three True Stories

**TP** THE TOWNSEND LIBRARY

For more titles in the Townsend Library,
visit our website: www.townsendpress.com

Photography: Beth Johnson

Townsend Press, Inc.
439 Kelley Drive
West Berlin, New Jersey 08091

ISBN-13: 978-1-59194-058-6
ISBN-10: 1-59194-058-3

Library of Congress Control Number:
2005934576

# Contents

*N*obody intends to become an addict.

Nobody takes his first drink, pops her first pill, or snorts her first line thinking, "I plan on getting hooked on this."

Instead, people tend to think things like this: "Addiction happens to other people." "Addicts are homeless people who live in the gutter." "Only weak-willed people get addicted," or "If I feel myself starting to get addicted, I'll stop."

The three people profiled in this book all had thoughts like that. Even after addiction had begun to control their lives, they told themselves that other people were addicts, not them. There were always excuses. John Ralston reasoned that as long as he drank and used cocaine only on the weekends, he wasn't hooked. Gwen Byrd told herself that crack wasn't so bad; it helped her get her housework done fast. Miguel Calbillo told himself that as long as he didn't put a needle in his arm, he wasn't a junkie.

Eventually, John, Gwen, and Miguel all had to face the truth: they are addicts, now addicts in recovery. No, they are not stereotypical junkies, panhandling in the street and nodding off in a doorway. Like most addicts, they are ordinary people. They are intelligent. They are educated. They are likeable. They did not foresee their lives heading in this direction.

They are typical as well in the way their addictions progressed. All three experimented with other substances before they found their "drug of choice": the one to which they were primarily addicted. John used alcohol, marijuana, and methamphetamines before developing his cocaine habit. Gwen used pot and cocaine before becoming hooked on crack. Miguel experimented with just about everything before becoming addicted to heroin.

And all three have paid a high price for their years of addiction. John's addiction cost him a marriage, his professional reputation, and his relationship with a person he deeply respected. Gwen's has cost her the custody of a child, her home, and much of her self-respect. Miguel finds himself, at thirty-one, just beginning to live a normal adult life.

To a person who has never experienced addiction, it can be hard to understand, frustrating, even irritating. You may want to ask, "Why didn't they just *stop*? This stuff was ruining their lives—couldn't they see that?" And true enough, it would have been a very good thing if John, Gwen, and Miguel had "just stopped" long ago.

But listening to their stories, a non-addict begins to comprehend the real horror of addiction. Every day further into an addiction, an addict loses a little more— more time, more self-respect, more opportunities.

It's a little like slipping down the side of an icy mountain, a few more inches every day. By the time the addict looks up toward the top of that mountain, the climb back seems overwhelmingly difficult. In order to get serious about quitting—starting that long climb back up—the addict has to honestly face all she has lost to her addiction. Those losses can include time, relationships, jobs, family, health, self-esteem, and more. The pain of confronting those thoughts begins to seem unbearable. And always in the back of the addict's mind is a little voice saying, "But you don't *have* to bear those thoughts! Snort a line! Pop a pill! Shoot up! Take a drink! Smoke a rock! And all the bad thoughts will go away. You can feel good again."

Yes, the addict can feel good again—for a little while. But then the drugs will wear off, and he will have slipped a few inches further down that mountainside. He looks up, sees the mountaintop even further in the distance, and the cycle continues.

# Introduction

But recovery is possible. For every promising future lost to addiction, there is a story of a person who faced his pain and fear, moved through it, and climbed that mountain.

Few people can do it alone. The recovering addict needs the support of peers who understand the pull of addiction as well as the sweetness of recovery. For many addicts, taking the step of asking for such support can be by far the hardest step in their journey toward wellness.

Almost every community in America offers some type of support for people struggling to overcome addictions. A local phone book will have listings (probably under "alcohol and drug abuse") in its local guide to human services. Any doctor should be able to refer a person struggling with addiction to local support groups or treatment centers. Alcoholics Anonymous, the most widely known addiction support group, offers daily meetings through the United States and world. Its sister organization, Narcotics

Anonymous, offers similar meetings for people addicted to drugs. LifeRing, the organization that John Ralston credits with supporting his sobriety, is becoming popular throughout the country. For anyone looking for a place to begin the road to recovery, the websites of these three organizations are an excellent place to start:

Alcoholics Anonymous:

**www.alcoholics-anonymous.org**

Narcotics Anonymous: **www.na.org**

LifeRing: www.unhooked.com

In addition, John Ralston, the volunteer leader of a LifeRing meeting in his community, has offered his e-mail address to anyone who wants to communicate with him about a substance abuse problem:

John Ralston: **doinfine@montco.biz**

If you yourself are struggling with addiction, the message of these stories is simple: *It is not too late.* Tomorrow will come. It can be one more day of addiction, or it can be the start of your new life.

If you are experimenting with drugs and alcohol but are not yet addicted, the message is simple as well: Do not invite the horror of addiction into your life.

And if you are a recovering addict: Keep on climbing that mountain. Don't look back. As John, Gwen, and Miguel can attest, every step gets a little easier.

# John

**John Ralston**

*A*ddicts sometimes talk about "hitting bottom"—reaching a point where they can no longer ignore the devastating effects of their habit. An addict in recovery can often point to one particular time and place where he hit bottom and was forced to confront some very ugly truths.

John Ralston knows exactly when he hit bottom: August 13, 2000 at 2:30 a.m. At that moment he was sitting in the driveway outside his mother's home. The spinning lights atop a police cruiser illuminated the quiet, small-town Pennsylvania neighborhood. A crowd of angry teenagers was approaching. John's bewildered mother was out on the lawn in her nightgown, crying and arguing with the officers. John was praying that his fourteen-year-old son would stay asleep inside the house. And piercing the fog of his confused, panicky, alcohol- and cocaine-soaked thinking was one screaming question: *"How in the world did I reach this point?"*

The John Ralston story was not supposed to include an episode like this. John was not supposed to be, at age thirty-eight, addicted, unemployed, and living with his mother. As a youngster, John was an intense, focused student who dreamed of college and a future as an architect. "I thought something big was coming," he says. "I didn't know what, exactly, but I expected a lot out of my life." He was inspired by the example of his stepfather, a retired military man who worked as a supervisor at a tool and die company. "I admired the heck out of him," John remembers. "He was a very solid guy, matter-of-fact and hard-working, but he had a really nice light side too." For example, his stepfather had decided that he wanted to learn to

# John

At age 43, John can smile and enjoy the simple pleasures of life, such as a fast-food lunch. It wasn't always that way.

paint. "So he took a course they had on PBS television and started painting beautiful landscapes, just because he had an interest.

"He was the wisest man I ever knew—although we used to kid him that he wasn't too smart to have married a woman with four children," John adds with a grin. "When I think of the responsibility he took on with us, I really am grateful to him."

John and his siblings were instantly absorbed by his stepfather's "very big, very Irish, very Catholic" family. "They were a stereotypical Irish family," John says with a chuckle, "into your business, expecting to know everything about you. It was overwhelming at first—and to be honest, sometimes it still is. But they were all loving, great people."

Despite plenty of family support, as he got into his senior year in high school, John, in his words, "lost focus."

"I began to hang around with different people," he remembers. "We drank and smoked pot and skipped school a lot. Somehow my thoughts about college and the future took a back seat to being part of this 'club.' That's what it felt like—that we pot-smokers had our little club, and I liked the feeling of belonging.

"But as with any drug, there was a price to pay for smoking pot," John says. "The effects started to linger. My memory got fuzzy. I'd always prided myself on being sharp, intelligent, and I wasn't so much anymore. That hurt my self-esteem. But instead of stopping, I used more."

His grades fell; he stopped talking about college. His parents noticed the change in him, but because he had always excelled at school they assumed it was "just a phase" that he'd pull out of. Instead, he and his favorite pot-smoking buddy Mike kicked it up a notch. One afternoon while they were smoking with an older couple in the neighborhood, the other people pulled out some white powder. It was methamphetamine.

"I said no at first, but they did a little arm-twisting—very little, if you want to know the truth," John says. "I didn't want to look silly by not trying it." He snorted his first line of meth. He hated the way it felt—"it burned my nose as if I had snorted battery acid"—but he loved the effect.

"Meth was the opposite of pot," he said. "Instead of slowing my thoughts down, this made me feel enlightened. A flood of ideas poured into my mind. I thought meth made me brilliant."

After high school graduation, John went to work at a poultry processing plant, cutting up chickens and turkeys and partying every weekend. After a year, he was fired after calling in "sick" one Monday too many. A few odd jobs followed until, at age nineteen, he enrolled in an eighteen-month program to learn the printing trade. Soon he was working in a print shop in Philadelphia.

He had acquired a new set of friends by then: hard-partying rock musicians who shared his increasingly ravenous taste for alcohol and meth. "I thought those two were the perfect combination," he says.

John works on designing a website. During his period of house detention, such design work helped keep him occupied.

"No matter how tired I was, the meth would bring me up. No matter how long I had been drinking, with meth I could drink more. I'd stay up for several days at a stretch."

John was still living at home, but his parents were not aware of the extent of his substance use. "They never saw me on weekends, and I didn't use during the week," he explains. "I thought that meant I didn't have a problem. A lot of addicts justify themselves that way—they say 'I only party on weekends,' or 'I always show up at work' or whatever. It's a way to try to minimize to yourself what you are doing. But the fact was that by Friday, I was completely preoccupied by how and where I was going to get my drugs. Drinking was not enough anymore. I had to have meth."

He was fired from his print-shop job after not showing up one day. "I don't remember the specifics, but I'm sure it was a Monday and I'm sure I lied about the reason," he says. "Deception was becoming more and more ingrained into my life. You know the old joke, 'How can you tell if an addict is lying? His lips are moving.' That's pretty close to the truth. Addicts lie as a way of life. You lie about things people aren't even asking you about. You're constantly making up stories to explain your behavior."

Living with his parents and doing local part-time jobs, John then met a neighborhood girl. He was twenty-three; she was eighteen. She was from a strict Baptist family and was, according to John, "pretty naïve about my weekend activities." Soon she was pregnant. She and John married a month before their son Jeremy was born.

The marriage was rocky from the start. John continued to drink and use drugs on the weekends. "We argued a lot. I was no treat, that's for sure," he remembers. "Sometimes I'd head out on Friday night and not show up until Sunday afternoon." After five years, his wife divorced him. Surprisingly, he convinced her to give him custody of Jeremy.

"I guess I snowed her," John says matter-of-factly. "I've always been a good salesman. I did have a good job at the time and worked very hard all week.

"And Jeremy—he's the one thing I've loved through all of this mess. He's been my saving grace.

"I admit there were way too many times I sent him to stay with my mom and stepfather for the weekends, weekends that I should have been with

John and Jeremy show off one of their giant-sized portraits.
This is one of the scientist Albert Einstein.

him," John says. "They were crazy about him and he had a great time, but that doesn't mean it was right. I should have been doing the father thing."

John did "the father thing" during the week, but weekends found him still partying with his musician friends. He had recently found a new love: cocaine.

"My buddy's band was popular in the Allentown

area," he recalls. "I'd often go hang out backstage where they were playing. One night, it was my birthday, and I was celebrating. I even got up on stage and sang with them.

"I'd done coke many times before, and it hadn't done anything for me. But on this particular night, I did a huge quantity, and this whole euphoria thing started in. I felt like I could do anything."

From that evening on, John was a cokehead.

"I loved my meth," John said with a shake of his head. "But the coke habit was worse. I don't think about meth anymore, but to this day I have thoughts about doing coke. I have to very deliberately take myself through the steps, remember all the repercussions that happened because of coke, so that I don't ever, ever get in that situation again.

"I won't say I didn't enjoy it, because I did," he admits. "I had some very fun times. But it'll kill you. I mean that in a spiritual and physical sense. You want more and more and more, and there isn't time enough or money enough in the world for it."

For a while, John continued in the pattern he'd been in for years—staying sober during the week, and partying all weekend. "Things went on like that between the time I was twenty-five and thirty-two," he recalls. "But then things started to change." Long-term cocaine use frequently leads to paranoid, even psychotic, behavior. This is the effect it began to have on John.

"I didn't want to go party with my friends," he recalls. "I didn't want to be with other people; all I wanted was my coke. I wanted to stay home and have it all to myself. I became paranoid to the point of insanity. I'd sit in a room with the curtains drawn, all alone, doing my lines, certain that the cops were going to break down the door any minute. My heart was pounding like a drum while I was thinking, 'Maybe this is the weekend that I'll have a heart attack and die. Someone will have to break the door down and find my body.' It was a very, very scary experience." He adds with a wry smile, "It was definitely not fun anymore."

Eventually the stress overwhelmed him. He broke down and went to his mother and stepfather, confessing how he had been living and saying, "I need help." With their encouragement, he approached his employer's human resources managers. He told them that he had a drinking problem. "That was true," he says today. "It would have been *more* true to say, 'And I'm doing a ton of cocaine,' but I didn't."

His employers were helpful; they had a "no questions asked" policy of helping troubled employees. They arranged for him to enter a twenty-eight-day rehab facility for substance abusers—seven days as an inpatient; twenty-one days outpatient.

At rehab, John was surprised to find many clients who, like him, had told half-truths to get there. "A lot of people check in supposedly for alcoholism alone, but once they are there they admit they're cross-addicted, like me," he says. "It's a lot more socially acceptable to tell your boss or your wife that you drink too much than that you're addicted to something like coke."

John threw himself into rehabilitation as he had once thrown himself into his schoolwork. "It was school again, and I was going to be the best!" he chuckles. He dutifully kept a journal; he participated in group discussion sessions. Once he was in the out-patient part of his program, he attended Alcoholics Anonymous (AA) meetings as his rehab counselors recommended.

There were some things he liked about AA. "I needed the support of my peers, and it was great to meet people from all walks of life who understood what it was to be addicted," he says. But there were other parts of AA that rubbed him the wrong way. For one thing, the organization has a strong spiritual tradi-tion; participants are expected to put their faith in a "higher power" that can help strengthen them. John, a non-religious man, felt uncomfortable with such talk.

# John

John relaxes at home with the family cats.

After six months of sobriety, he began to drink and use cocaine again.

"I still look at that rehab experience as valuable," he says. "Just because it didn't have long-term effects doesn't mean I didn't learn a lot. I just needed to learn a lot more."

John's education about addiction continued. Late one night he left the apartment of a woman he was dating, angry about an argument they'd had. He got in his car and roared out onto the highway for the ten-mile drive home.

"I was a very aggressive driver when I was drinking and using coke," he says. "I should have been arrested dozens, maybe hundreds of times."

This time he was. He had almost reached his home when he saw a police car coming after him. He pulled into his development, parked, and ran in his front door, hoping to disappear. But two officers were right behind him, and he found himself an unwilling participant in the Driving Under the

# John

Influence (DUI) experience.

"They handcuffed me; they took me to the hospital; they drew my blood for a blood test, and then they took me home," he remembers.

"The next day I honestly managed not to think about it for a half-day or so," he says. "But as the cobwebs cleared, I thought, 'Maybe the papers won't print my name in the arrest file,' or 'Maybe because I was so nice and cooperative to the cops, they'll just let it slide.'"

But there was his name in the paper. "And then everything started," John says. "A DUI is really the gift that keeps on giving." He ticks off a few of the next steps: "I go to my arraignment. Later my sentencing day comes along. A judge says, 'You are guilty,' I'm handcuffed with a bunch of other criminals and taken under the courthouse to the prison, where I'm fingerprinted and photographed. The fines and fees cost me a couple of thousand dollars. I lost my license for thirty days. There I am, thirty-six

John and Denise met online, through a service that brings people in recovery together.

years old, and I'm having to ask people for rides everywhere I want to go."

He had to deal with his son, Jeremy, who was then twelve. "I told him the basics, but what was I gonna say?" John says. "I was so stuck in my own shame. He loved me and I loved him, but I was definitely not ready to lead by example."

Rather than using his arrest as a wake-up call, John plunged even deeper into his addictions. It was only when he was drunk and high that he could forget his growing shame and self-loathing. He began drinking more heavily than ever; he used "mega amounts" of cocaine, and his paranoia was "over the moon." He was dating women he'd meet at bars, the relationships revolving around the participants' addictions. "They were people like me, drug-users with self-esteem problems," he recalls. "You try to have a relationship in conditions like that, and you've got something really toxic on your hands." He was working only now and then. While he had once held high-paying union jobs, doing skilled printing work, a reputation for being unreliable was now following him. When he was working at all, it was at low-end work, doing the manual labor in print shops.

"My weekends were getting longer, and they interfered with my ability to work," he says drily. One of those weekends found him giving the eulogy at the funeral of Michael, his original pot-smoking and meth-snorting buddy. After years of living in his own hell of addiction, Michael had shot himself in the head.

Two more years went by. It was early the morning of August 13, 2000. John was driving home from his favorite local bar, where he'd been drinking and snorting cocaine. He was out of work and out of money, to the point where he and Jeremy had moved in with his mother. John's stepfather had died by then. To his shame, John was not on good terms with the man at the end of his life.

"He called me on how I was living," John remembers. "He saw through my excuses and my lies. He knew I was living week by week, blowing all my money, not saving for my son's college, not putting anything away for retirement. He called me on it all, so I distanced myself from him." He shakes his head sadly. "It was the time I needed him in my life most, but I pushed him away."

John rounded a corner, pulled into the street

where his mother lived, and plowed directly into the back of a parked car. The car contained a group of teenage boys, and they poured out of the vehicle, shaken and angry. Drunken and vulnerable, John didn't want them to catch him. So he kept driving.

"Of course, the cops were there instantly, as I pulled into my mother's driveway," he said. "It was such a horror show. I can't even describe the humiliation. My mother comes out of the house and finds me handcuffed in the back of a cop car. The neighbors are looking out their windows. Mom is trying to argue with the cops, while I'm sitting there saying, 'Please, please tell her to stop. I'm OK.' I'm praying Jeremy will stay asleep inside the house. All I can think of is, 'Now I'm dragging other people into this.'"

Over the course of the next few weeks, John discovered that his first DUI was a walk in the park compared to his second. This time, he lost his license for a year. He was given thirty days home detention, with no exceptions—he could not leave the house for any reason. He was charged a fifteen hundred dollar fine, plus court and probation costs. At his mother's insistence, he hired a lawyer for another fifteen hundred dollars, but the lawyer could do nothing for him—his blood test showed an alcohol count that was well over the legal limit.

Home detention, John discovered, was its own kind of masterpiece of humiliation. At any hour of the day or night, the telephone in his mother's house might ring. John had to answer it. When he did, a recorded call from the probation office asked him to read off a list of the US states. A computerized voice analysis then determined whether or not he was intoxicated.

"The phone could ring at 3 a.m.," John says. "It could ring while my mother had friends over. Only I could answer the phone. The whole family was dragged into my mess."

Facing the prospect of thirty days inside the house, with no alcohol or drugs, John realized he had to find something to keep him busy. He persuaded his mother to let him finish her unfinished basement. She bought the materials, and he went to work framing and dry-walling. He turned to his computer and began experimenting with setting up websites, eventually beginning a small website-design business.

The court ordered him to attend twelve AA meetings. His mother had to drive him there. Once again, he didn't find the organization a good fit. "There was lots of dogma, lots of religious orientation, which is fine if people want it, but I didn't," he says. "But I knew that if I was ever going to be sober, I needed to find a peer group. So I began looking online."

Eventually, John read about a California-based recovery group called LifeRing. There were no LifeRing meetings in his area of Pennsylvania, so he began to attend "virtual" meetings online and learn all he could about the organization.

LifeRing was completely secular, not religious. In contrast to AA's motto, "One day at a time,"

LifeRing's is, "Don't drink, no matter what." That approach appealed to John.

"For me, someone who finally wanted to live my life and make plans, I liked the idea that I could look ahead a month, a year, and assume that I'd be sober then," he said. "And I couldn't make God my way to be sober."

Sitting alone at his computer in his mother's home, reading about LifeRing and the experience of other recovering addicts, John began to feel a glimmer of hope and excitement. He was also terrified.

"I'd been through this DUI thing before, so this time I knew exactly what to expect," he says. "It had hurt my ego a lot, a whole lot, to get into this position a second time, and this time it was affecting my whole family. I couldn't stuff it away and deal with it privately anymore. I had to face the fact that my entire life was unraveling."

As he considered the steps he could take toward sobriety, John realized one thing for sure: he could

# John

The pamphlets in John's hand are from LifeRing, the addiction support group that helps him stay sober.

no longer hang around with his old drinking and drugging buddies. After his arrest—even before his home detention began—he cut ties with them all.

"I basically cut fifty people out of my life in one day," he said. "If they called, I'd make excuses—'I can't go out; I don't have any money.' Pretty soon they vanished. I had to let them go. I had to give up a lot of people and places if I was going to change my life."

When his home detention period was over, John stayed deeply involved with the online LifeRing community, relying heavily on its support and encouragement. His days of sobriety stretched into weeks, then months, then a year. When he had been sober for eighteen months, he felt great about his accomplishment. He also felt lonely.

"I thought, 'Maybe I could handle dating now.'" He posted a personals ad on a website called "Recoveringmates.com," designed for recovering substance abusers. He got a response from a woman named Denise.

# John

"We e-mailed for probably three months," John recalls. "I told her everything about me, but she was very protective about her personal information. I really liked her, but I didn't even know where she was. Finally she agreed to go out with me. Then I learned she lived six miles from my house."

Denise and John met and instantly clicked. It turned out that Denise, too, had discovered LifeRing online and had depended on the organization to help her achieve sobriety. As the two became more deeply involved, they decided to establish a "real-world" LifeRing chapter in their own area. The local public library offered a room, and John and Denise became the hosts of a weekly meeting.

Both of them praise the useful, nuts and bolts skills that LifeRing emphasizes. "Every meeting begins with the question, 'How was your week?'" John says. "From there we go on to talk about very practical stuff—such as, 'How am I going to get home from work without passing "my" bar?' or

'What do I do when my co-workers want me to go out for a beer after work? How do I say "no"? Or am I confident enough in my sobriety to go along and have a Coke?'"

After dating for two years, John and Denise got married. They now own a pretty home with a spacious, tree-shaded backyard. John is working as an ads salesman for the local newspaper, as well as doing web design on the side. Jeremy is a nineteen-year-old college student, studying graphic arts. He and his father have taken on an unusual hobby together.

"A big part of being sober is figuring out how to fill your time," John explains. "If you're not on that bar stool, where are you going to be? So one day, Jeremy and I were sitting around and I started thinking about my stepfather's painting. I said to Jeremy, 'How cool would it be to make a big 8 by 8-foot painting of Einstein?!' I've always liked Einstein; he was smart and had a good sense of humor.

"Jeremy looked at me like I was crazy, but I

dragged him off to Home Depot and we got boards and used my multi-media projector to project a photograph of Einstein on them. Then we traced over the lines and basically created a huge paint-by-number image. We started painting it, and then I said, 'Hey, how cool would it be to finish the painting at the Sunday in the Park concert?!'" John was referring to a popular local concert series in the community park. "Jeremy was horrified, but I sent out press releases, and we made the front pages of the local papers." Since then, the father-and-son team have produced several other giant portraits.

With five years of sobriety under his belt, John Ralston sounds like a contented man. "For Denise and me, things just keep getting better," he says. "Being sober, we can do things together that would not have been possible before. We can plan and travel and accomplish whatever we set our minds to.

"And Jeremy is great. I talk to him about my addiction; I warn him of the potential there. Now I

John, Jeremy, and Denise are looking together toward a
happy, healthy future.

feel I can talk to him as a father ought to talk to his
son. I've got a leg to stand on. I can't undo the
things that I've done, so I just tell him the truth and
hope that he'll learn from it. He's got a spark in his
eye like I did at his age. I tell him, he can accomplish
something big if he avoids the pitfalls I fell into."

Sitting on a deck chair under a shady tree in his

# John

backyard, holding hands with Denise, John speaks with deep appreciation of where he is now in his life.

"I had dreams once, but they faded from color to gray when I was trapped in my addictions," he says. "Now that I'm sober, my dreams have their color back."

# Gwen

**Gwen Byrd**

*G*wen Byrd sits in the food court of a mall near her home, nursing a cup of coffee through a long morning. She is telling a stranger about her life.

Gwen and her interviewer had planned to talk in a nearby park, but the day is rainy, forcing them to find a dry spot indoors. There isn't room to meet where Gwen is now living, a room at a Howard Johnson's motel. She shares the space with her twelve-year-old son, Darryl. Gwen and Darryl have been at the motel for close to a year now. Gwen doesn't mind it so much for herself, but it has been tough on Darryl. He has gone through the entire sixth grade with a motel room as his home. His school bus driver kindly arranged to pick him up first in the morning and drop him off last in the afternoon, so that everyone wouldn't know he and his mom were living at Howard Johnson's. Of course, some kids found out anyway, and they teased Darryl.

Gwen and Darryl haven't always lived in a cheap motel room. Gwen hasn't always been on welfare, putting in volunteer hours at a Goodwill store and picking up meals at a soup kitchen in Camden, New Jersey. A bright, well-spoken woman with a high school degree and a year of college to her credit, Gwen can be capable and hard-working. She has been employed as a mailroom supervisor and then a slot-machine attendant at Atlantic City casinos. She's held an office job. She's worked as a head cashier at a BJ's Wholesale Club.

But it seems like a long time since Gwen was able to concentrate on getting a job, or keeping one once she had it. Since 1988, her life has been run not by the desire to keep a job, or take care of her children, or eat or sleep regularly, or pay her bills, or have a

Gwen and Darryl sit in their cramped motel room, their home
for nearly a year.

nice home. It hasn't been driven by any of the needs
or desires that motivate most people. Instead, it has
been driven by the all-consuming need for crack.

Crack is cocaine that has been chemically altered
to make it smokable. (Cocaine itself is a powder that
is usually inhaled.) It is sold in the form of little rock-
like nuggets. The name "crack" comes from the
crackling sound the rocks make as they burn.

Crack is widely believed to be the most addictive
substance ever developed. Gwen can testify to that.

Darryl

She hadn't been any angel before she began using crack. She'd fooled around with other drugs. But crack was something else altogether. From her first hit, it had her in its grip. "Crack came before paying the bills. Before eating. Before sleeping. Before going to work," she says, "It became my air, my vitamins, my medicine.

"And I regret it all," she says, her bitter expression making her appear older than her forty-five years. "Crack has torn my life apart."

Gwen was born in December, 1959 in Bridgeton, New Jersey. She was the third of her mother's four children, each with a different father. Gwen's mother couldn't afford a place big enough to keep all the children together, so the four were farmed out to various friends and relatives. Gwen lived with her godparents, an older man and woman. With them she was quiet, studious, a "church girl" with a good reputation.

But when Gwen was thirteen, her mother got married, and Gwen's stepfather bought a five-bedroom house where the whole family could live. "They threw us together and expected us to be the Brady Bunch," Gwen remembers. The problem was, the four siblings barely knew one another and didn't much care to change that. Meanwhile, their mother and new stepfather began to brawl; Gwen's mother once slashed his neck so badly he needed eight-nine stitches. Her mother also learned the startling fact that she was his seventh wife. Gwen was surprised and confused by the lessons her mother began teaching her and her two sisters. "She basically taught us to be whores," she recalls. "She'd tell us, 'If you're gonna be with a man, you get something out of it. Don't be a fool and give it away.'

"She worked hard as a domestic," Gwen goes on. "She had only a sixth grade education, and I appreciate how hard she worked to support us. But she instilled values in us that I hate to this day."

Unhappy at home, Gwen began to drift away to hang with her own friends. Drinking and smoking marijuana helped her feel like she was part of the crowd. The interest she had had in school when she was living with her godparents evaporated, and she got involved in shoplifting and even stealing cars for thrills. Her stepfather vanished, and Gwen and her siblings got jobs to help their mother afford the house payments.

Gwen's natural intelligence helped her maintain average grades even though she did not work hard in school. She never thought of college, but as her high school graduation grew near, her mother and father and godparents surprised her by saying they wanted her to go, and that they would help her pay for it. "I didn't want to go," she says. "I had a job and a car. I was running the streets and getting high, and I didn't know why I had to do anything different." But when she was admitted to Cheyney University in Pennsylvania on probationary status, she began to feel a little excited about the prospect.

She started school, doing pretty well, but then began spending more time hanging out with her cousin Judy than attending classes. The two liked to go to the clubs where Judy worked as an exotic dancer—in other words, a stripper. Gwen enjoyed flirting, drinking, and dancing at the clubs, occasionally doing lines of cocaine. Then one night one of the strippers didn't show up. The club manager said to Judy, "Hey, why doesn't your cousin go on?"

Gwen sputtered, "I can't be a stripper!"

The manager said, "Sure you can. I've seen you dance; you've got style. Just do the same thing, only take your clothes off while you do it." Then the manager peeled off three one hundred dollar bills and put them in Gwen's hand.

"I said to the bartender, 'Give me a triple shot,'" Gwen says. "I drank it down and went on stage."

Gwen dropped out of college and worked as a stripper for two years. At first she regarded it as an exciting adventure that wasn't hurting anyone. "I figured I was this country girl doing something nobody from Bridgeton had ever done before," she remembers. She made good money. Men were glad to buy her drinks and cocaine. Then they began asking her to meet them away from work for "dates"—dates

In spite of their difficulties, Gwen and Darryl are still close.

which they would pay for. "It started out fun, but the job turned me into a whore," she says matter-of-factly. "I wasn't walking the streets, but it amounted to the same thing."

She began dating the manager of a club and quit working, allowing him to support her. But when she found out he was married, she broke the relationship off. After that she worked for a while as a nanny for a wealthy family. That ended after she passed the security code for the house to some friends for five hundred dollars, which she spent on coke and marijuana. When the friends later burglarized the house, Gwen's employers suspected she was involved, but they fired her without pressing charges.

"I look back at the crazy things I did, and I'm so embarrassed," she says. "At the center of every one of them was drugs. I was just stupid, stupid for drugs."

She took her first job at an Atlantic City casino, working in the mailroom. Soon she became involved with Paul, a drug dealer. "I thought, 'What a great idea! Why buy drugs when I can go with a dealer?'" Gwen soon discovered that life with Paul was painful; soon after they began dating, he beat her so badly he broke her jaw. While she was recovering from her injuries she found that she was pregnant. When she told Paul, he took off for Florida.

Gwen remembers the early months of her pregnancy as an oasis of sanity in a life that was slipping out of control. As soon as she had learned she was pregnant, she stopped using drugs and drinking. She was sharing an apartment with a girlfriend, and had a circle of close female friends. "They used drugs," she admits, "but they totally supported me not using. They were excited about the baby, too. They'd tell me, 'Well, it won't have a daddy, but it'll have a whole lot of moms.'" She went to work, stayed clean, enjoyed shopping for baby clothes and furniture, and waited for the baby's arrival.

Then one day when she was visiting her mother, she looked up to see Paul at the door. "He went into the whole, 'Oh, baby, baby, I was so wrong, we belong together' bit, and I fell for it," she says, disgust in her voice. "I was glad to think the baby would have a daddy after all."

Only a week after Paul's arrival, Gwen went into labor, just six and a half months into her pregnancy. Her son weighed only a little over three pounds. He spent two and one-half months in the hospital, with

Darryl looks out their only window.

Gwen sleeping on a recliner chair outside the nursery.

When the baby was able to leave the hospital, Gwen moved back into her apartment with her girl-friend and returned to work at the casino. Paul watched the baby during her first day back at work, and she picked up her son on her way home. "Paul said he'd call or come by later that night," Gwen remembers, her eyes beginning to glaze with tears at the memory. "I took the baby to the store and then back to the apartment. In Atlantic City, it gets breezy in the evening out on the boardwalk, and I remember thinking, 'It's too windy to have a little baby out here.' So we went inside."

Gwen fed the baby and lay down to sleep on the bed next to him. When she next woke, it was nearly 1 a.m. "I thought, 'Paul never called,'" she remembers. "Then I thought, 'The baby is beginning to sleep longer.'" She reached out to pat her son, but he didn't respond to her touch. She rolled him over and found he wasn't breathing.

Gwen grabbed the baby and ran the five blocks to the nearby hospital, where doctors tried to revive him. But there was nothing they could do. The baby had died of SIDS—Sudden Infant Death Syndrome.

Paul and Gwen's relationship did not survive the death of their son. (She learned that he had been out with another woman the night the baby died.) Gwen broke down mentally; when her mother found her pretending that a Cabbage Patch Doll was her baby son, she called an ambulance. Gwen ended up in a psychiatric hospital for several weeks.

After leaving the hospital, Gwen returned to Atlantic City and her casino job, but it was as if something had broken inside her. She blamed herself for her son's death, wondering if her drug use had caused his health problems. She became involved with yet another abusive man, this one an alcoholic, and was soon pregnant again. Soon after her baby girl, Ebony, was born in 1988, she attended a July 4th cookout with the baby's father. A cousin of his brought crack. She asked for a hit.

"Everyone reacts differently to crack," Gwen says. "Some sit and act real quiet. Me, I have to move. Right away I felt paranoid and had to go check on the baby.

I heard them say to my boyfriend, 'Why'd your girl take a hit and go flying out of the room like that?'"

Besides feeling paranoid and jumpy, Gwen had another powerful response to crack: "As soon as I smoked that rock I wanted more. I wanted it *immediately*, that second.

"And so that monster was out of the box."

And a monster it was. Within weeks, the drug was the center of Gwen's life. How to get more, where to buy it, how to keep enough on hand, where to smoke it without getting caught—these were the thoughts that obsessed her. Her boyfriend had begun using too, and the effect on him was devastating.

"Ebony's father—when he's sober, he's one of the best men I've ever known," she says. "He's responsible and hard-working and a perfect father. But when he smokes crack and drinks, it's like it releases a devil in him."

For instance, one evening when they'd been on the pipe, Gwen and he went out to buy beer. She was

The park offers a change of scene from Gwen and Darryl's room.

standing at the store counter while her boyfriend stood some yards away. "I was asking the cashier for the beer, but he imagined I was making a date with the guy," she says. "So he jumped up, punched me hard in the face, and proceeded to tear the store apart."

Time went on. Gwen continued to work in Atlantic City. Ultimately she worked at five different casinos for a total of ten years. When she could stay clean she was an excellent employee—smart, capable, quick. But crack binges made her increasingly undependable.

"When you're on crack, you don't eat and you don't sleep," she says. "You get dehydrated and sick. It sucks everything out of you." On several occasions, she passed out at work and was sent to the hospital. When blood tests revealed drugs in her system, she was fired.

She lost other jobs for different drug-related reasons. At one casino, she had taken the course to become a slot-machine attendant. It was a good job, but she got greedy. Not only did she begin selling coke to her fellow employees, she was skimming money off the top of the slot-machine take.

One day auditors walked into her office to conduct a surprise inspection of the books. She panicked. Not only did she fear that the records would reveal her theft, but her bag of cocaine was in the same desk drawer as the books.

"An auditor was standing right there, waiting for the books," she said. "I did everything to avoid opening the drawer. I even knocked a lamp off the desk to try to distract him. He finally snatched the drawer open himself, and there was the coke, in plain sight."

Gwen denied that the coke was hers. There was no lock on the drawer, so it wasn't clear that she had put it there. Rather than call the police, the casino management fired not only Gwen but all the other staffers who had access to the desk.

Gwen moved on. She left Ebony's father and took a job at a Philadelphia truck-driving school, where she helped students arrange financial aid. She was living with yet another man, this one who was in recovery from addiction. With his encouragement, she stopped using for a while. But his brother was a dealer. One day, the dealer took Gwen aside and asked if she'd like to make an extra one hundred dollars a day passing out packets of drugs to the runners on the corner near her office. She agreed.

One morning not much later, Gwen came out of the house, intending to take Ebony to day care before going to work. She heard a commotion and saw the dealer running toward her. He gasped out that the police were chasing him and tossed her a bag. "Hide it for me," he said, and he was gone.

Gwen stuffed the bag in Ebony's stroller and kept walking. When she was out of sight of the cops, she opened the bag. Inside were six large bundles of crack.

"I lost it," she admits. Pushing her baby's stroller, she kept on going, blindly, her mind reeling. It was December and snowing lightly. On and on she walked, with no plan in mind except to find a safe place to get high. Eventually she saw a couple of people in front of a run-down house.

"I didn't know those people from a can of paint," she says. "but I said, 'Do you know where I can go to get high?' They thought I was asking where I could buy drugs. 'I said, no, I *have* drugs. I just need a place.'"

The people let her into the house in exchange for some of the drugs.  For the next three days she smoked crack steadily, occasionally giving someone money to go out to buy food or diapers for Ebony.

After three days, as the smoke cleared from the crack pipe and her head, Gwen realized she was in trouble. The dealer was going to come looking for her and the drugs. She panicked and fled back to Atlantic City, where she ended up in a homeless shelter with the baby. The unraveling of her life picked up speed. Ebony's father sued for custody. When his petition failed, his sister sued instead. Social services demanded a urine test from Gwen. When it turned up "dirty," the sister got temporary custody.

Gwen stopped using long enough to get Ebony back. Over the years, she has stopped using briefly many times. But the desire for the drug is too strong. "When I don't use, I get pissed off. I'm depressed. I get crying spells, and I'm angry, and I begin thinking about all the things in my life I've screwed up." Eventually the desire to escape those thoughts overwhelms her, and she takes another hit.

"The best comparison to crack addiction I've ever heard is this," Gwen continues. "It's as if you're in a room on a stinking hot, sticky day. You're miserable and sweaty, and there's an air conditioner sitting right there. All you have to do to get a cool breeze is turn that air conditioner on. Just press the button, that's all! But the breeze only lasts for a few minutes, and you have to do it again, and again, and again.

"And for what?" Gwen asks, despair in her voice. "For nothing! You get nothing out of it. Nothing but misery and loss."

A few years later, Ebony was five and living again with her mother. Gwen had hooked up with a heroin addict. One evening after a day of hustling unsuccessfully for drugs, he was sick and strung out and demanded money from Gwen. With an addict's logic, she told him no. "I said that I'd share my crack with him, but that heroin wasn't my thing, and I wasn't going to give him money to buy something I didn't even use." He became violent, and tried to take the cash he knew she had hidden in her bra. As Ebony watched, Gwen picked up a pair of scissors and stabbed him deep in the chest.

With her boyfriend hovering between life and death with a collapsed lung, Gwen went to jail, charged with assault with a deadly weapon and endangering a minor. Ebony's aunt filed a petition for permanent custody, citing Gwen's violent behavior. The hearing was scheduled during Gwen's time in prison. Gwen loved her daughter and wanted Ebony with her. But she knew what kind of impression she would make

# Gwen

Gwen is searching for an affordable apartment where she and Darryl can move.

showing up at the hearing wearing shackles and her orange prison jumpsuit. She let Ebony's aunt take custody.

A few days later she received a call to report to the prison infirmary. There she was informed that she was eight weeks pregnant.

"I said to the guard, 'Just give me your damn gun so I can blow my brains out. I'm thirty-three, I'm locked up, I just lost my child, and I'm pregnant.'"

Her boyfriend recovered, and Gwen got out of jail on probation. She was ordered into the first of the five recovery programs she has tried, and warned that if her baby was born with cocaine in its system, she would return to prison.

She didn't find the program effective. It was based in an area of Atlantic City where drugs were easy to come by. The schedule allowed her to be home early in the afternoon. After arriving home, the hours stretched out before her, begging to be filled with getting high. She smoked crack almost every night. The day she went into labor she had not only smoked but done lines of coke as well.

Like her other two children, Darryl was born prematurely. He weighed only three pounds. The day after his birth, Gwen was lying in her hospital bed when two Atlantic City police officers and a social worker entered the room. Frozen with fear, she watched them come—and go to the bed of the other new mother in her room. "They arrested her and told her they were taking the baby," Gwen said. "It was born addicted to heroin and was going through withdrawal. They took her into custody right then. She was crying and kept saying, 'I'm sorry, I'm sorry, I tried.' I wanted to jump out the window."

For reasons Gwen has never understood, her son had not tested positive for drugs. She went home with the baby.

For a short time, her fright over Darryl's birth kept her straight. But then she and a girlfriend moved back to her hometown, Bridgeton, and began their own drug business. One night someone pounded on the door, yelling, "Open up, this is a raid." Gwen thought it was a customer fooling around, as he often did. She threw open the door saying, "Curtis, knock it off"—when ten police officers entered the house, their guns drawn.

"They began searching the house," she said. "Darryl was almost two and sleeping in his crib in my bedroom. I knew if the cop threw open that door, it would hit the crib and he'd cry. I was scared to death they'd shoot him. So I said, 'Hold it, hold it, I'll give you what I have.'"

Gwen pleaded guilty to the drug charges. She could have been sentenced to five years in prison and a twenty-five hundred dollar fine. Instead, she was given a year's probation and a reduced fine, and was ordered into yet another recovery program. This was a three-month inpatient program. It was "brutal; militant," Gwen recalls. But it was effective. Counselors forced participants to talk about their most painful, shameful moments, even role-play them with other addicts. A mother who had left her children alone one night when their house burned was paired with a fire fighter who had been too high to go into a burning building where a child was trapped. Counselors forced them to stand in the middle of the room answering questions like, "Maria, why did you leave the kids alone like that? Where did you go? What did you do there?" and "John, what were you doing that left you so confused and messed-up? How did you feel when you learned that child had died?"

After leaving the program, Gwen stayed clean for almost two years.

Then she reunited with Darryl's father. He had been in and out of prison during her recovery. Now he came around, wanting a relationship with his son. Gwen was working while he stayed home and watched Darryl. He began getting high. One night Gwen arrived home to find he'd sold her television set for drug money. "I tried to beat him to death," Gwen admits, and then he was gone again, for good this time.

(When asked why she keeps getting involved with abusive, addicted men, Gwen struggles for words. Finally she says, "Stupidity. Loneliness. Thinking I can't get along with a man. Lots of excuses, none of them good.")

Again raising her child alone, depressed, and angry, Gwen was hitting bottom. Then she got a letter from Darryl's father, who was in jail again. "I need to tell you something," he wrote. "One of the people I used to shoot up with just died of AIDS. You and Darryl ought to get tested."

"I about lost my mind," she recalls. "I told my mother. You know how you go to your mother for some kind of support? Her response was, 'How stupid could you be?'"

She put off being tested for two months. During that time, she began using crack again. Her test and Darryl's came back negative, but then she failed a random urine test, violating the terms of her probation. She was ordered back into yet another outpatient program.

"This time, I said 'to hell with it,'" she recalls. "I left my son with my mother, and I went off on a nineteen-day binge."

Her run came to an end one morning at 4 a.m.

# Gwen

Darryl is a cheerful, high-spirited young man, but Gwen worries about the effect of her addiction on him.

when she returned to the crack house where she'd been crashing. Another addict said to her, "Your mom's been here. She gave me fifty dollars to tell her where you were."

Gwen knew her time had run out. "I got high and I started walking across town," she recounts. "I passed a trash can and threw away the rest of my drugs." She walked into a police station and said to the startled officer on duty, "You have a warrant for me. I'm high, I'm tired, and I can't do this anymore. I just want to lie down before my mother finds me and kills me."

Gwen was locked up briefly for probation violation, contempt of court, and failure to pay a fine. She was then ordered into yet another treatment program —an inpatient program at Seabrook House in Bridgeton. The MatriArk program is specifically designed for mothers in recovery and their children.

Gwen's mother dropped her off for her first day at Seabrook. The two women had always had a complicated relationship, but even Gwen was not prepared for her mother's goodbye. As they sat in the car in front of the hospital, Gwen's mother opened the glovebox and pulled out a handgun. Tapping it on Gwen's leg, she said, "Gwen, you're my daughter and I love you. But I can't take this anymore. Your children can't take it anymore. If you don't get yourself together, I will kill you. Now goodbye, and I'll come see you on visitors' day."

At Seabrook, Gwen says, "They broke me down from the beginning. They took my jewelry. They took my phone. The intake counselor said, 'This is not the Betty Ford clinic, so get over yourself now. You'll be allowed two ten-minute calls a week, and they won't be on your cell phone.' They made me deal with my manipulative attitude. They made me deal with everything."

Most painfully of all, they made her deal with the death of her baby son, something she had steadfastly refused to even let herself think about. When she refused to write a goodbye letter to her son, her counselor seemed to give up on the subject. But the next day when Gwen walked into her group counseling session, she found the room transformed into a funeral parlor. Organ music was playing; a white box with a baby doll stood on a table in the center of the room. The other mothers in recovery participated in

Fighting her crack addiction is a daily struggle for Gwen.

the baby's "funeral." One read a poem; another sang. At the end of the service, shaken to her core, Gwen helped bury the doll in a grassy spot behind the hospital.

# Gwen

Ebony came to visit. She told her mother, in front of the group, what it was like to have a crack addict for a mother. Gwen's mother came. The two women talked about their relationship before the group, and Gwen began to realize how passive and child-like she had always been with her mom. "With the drugs out of the way, I was finally able to stand up to her like an adult," Gwen says. "And our relationship has remained better to this day. When she starts in with, 'I told you so; how could you be so stupid,' I can say, 'Stop. Just stop. Don't go there. That isn't helpful.'"

After nine months, Gwen came out of Seabrook, reunited with Darryl, and tried again. She got a cashier's job and had found a decent place to live. Then a bus accident left her injured; three weeks later she was laid off her job. Unable to keep up her rental payments, she and Darryl were put out on the street. Gwen put their furniture and other belongings in storage, but ran out of money to pay the storage fee. She lost everything. Then came the welfare motel.

Under the stress, Gwen did what she's done for decades: she began using crack again.

"I'm struggling hard," she says. "I've started treatment. I'm looking for an apartment. We'll start all over again."

Her great fears are for her children. "I could get a place in Camden," she says, referring to the nearby New Jersey city that is notorious for drug use and violence, "but I can't do that to Darryl. I'd lose him there for sure."

So far, both Darryl and Ebony are doing all right. Both are B students. Darryl is going to summer camp this year, and he's become involved in a program that will match him with adult male mentors. Ebony is a "good girl," says her mother, but she also knows that Ebony has started drinking and defying her aunt's rules at home.

"If I found out that she was using drugs . . ." She chokes up at the thought and has to stop talking for a while. "If I found that out—first, I'd cry myself to

Gwen and Darryl talk about the summer camp he
will be attending.

death. Then I'd talk to her—not beat her down, but
talk to her. I'd tell her, 'Yeah, I've done this and I've
done that, and I'm ashamed and embarrassed about
those things. But I didn't have to do those things.
They were choices, and you don't have to make those
choices. I'm still here, just by the grace of God. I'm
here. But you might not make it through."

# Miguel

**Miguel Calbillo**

When Miguel Calbillo was a little boy in Houston, he saw a lot in his family that was good and admirable. His mother, a nurse, and his father, a television cameraman, were intelligent and creative people. They cared about others and were deeply involved in community activism. They fought for migrant workers' rights and against police brutality; they were active in the National Organization for Women and demonstrated for the Equal Rights Amendment. They loved the arts and encouraged Miguel and his older sister to read books, listen to music, visit museums, and see movies and plays.

"All those good things were visible on the surface," says Miguel, now thirty-one, "and we had some great times." But there was an aspect to their lives that wasn't as obvious, or as positive. That was Miguel's father's drug use.

"My dad was a multi-substance abuser, all my life," Miguel remembers. "He was a big drinker, and there was a lot of pot. He worked very long hours, fueled by cocaine." Miguel's parents argued with increasing bitterness about the drug use. Shouting eventually turned to violence, and they divorced when Miguel was four.

After the divorce, Miguel and his sister spent much of their time with their maternal grandmother while their mom worked two and even three jobs to support them. They saw their dad often, and Miguel began to realize that his father was often out of work. "He kept losing jobs," he remembers. "He'd move from one station to another, and he'd be wonderful, and then he'd screw up. Everyone he ever worked for

Miguel sits and thinks in a local park.

loved him; everyone tried to help him. They'd give him chance after chance after chance. They offered him anything—rehab, time off, whatever he needed. But it never worked. He'd eventually lose the job. I saw how hard my mom was working, and I began to resent that about him."

That was the beginning of what has been a long and conflicted relationship between Miguel and his father, whom he clearly admires. "My father is a brilliant person," Miguel says, "creative, well-read, well-traveled; a real force of nature. A very memorable, macho guy. I think everyone in Houston has a story about my father.

"But I didn't like the way he treated my mother, and I didn't like it that his drug use got in the way of holding a job. Very early on in life I decided that I didn't want to be like him in those negative ways.

"And the more I fought against them, the more of his mistakes I repeated."

Following both his parents' examples, Miguel became an enthusiastic reader at an early age. When he was still a preschooler, he learned to love the "underground comics" of artists like R. Crumb. "They were all about weirdos and geeks and losers like me," Miguel says with a laugh. "They made me feel better about being the skinny Hispanic kid with glasses who liked to read."

Classmates are rarely kind to a kid who seems different, and the "skinny Hispanic kid with glasses" came in for more than his share of abuse. To make matters worse, Miguel had such severe asthma that he was frequently hospitalized. Sometimes he had to be injected with adrenaline, which he remembers as "so awful. I'd seize up, have shakes and tremors and try to scream, but I couldn't because my teeth were clenched so tightly."

Feeling like a social reject and enduring health problems, Miguel looked for ways to make himself feel better. He found them close at hand. He'd attended concerts with his parents all his life, and by the time he was eight he was in the habit of draining the alcoholic drinks people had left on their tables. With his father smoking marijuana so frequently, he never lacked for a way to get high. "My uncles would blow pot smoke in my face," he remembers. "Or when I'd be on a long car trip, I'd sit in the back seat between two people who were passing a joint."

When he was eleven, his drug experimentation kicked up a notch. The city of Houston was holding a huge celebration as part of the Texas Sesquicentennial. A massive laser and fireworks show was the festival's centerpiece. Wandering around waiting for the show to start, Miguel observed his father buying some LSD. "I said, 'Hey, Dad, give me some,'" he remembers. "I think he was buying coke too, and he handed me a hit to get me to go away." Miguel lay down in the grass to watch the laser show as he took his first acid trip.

By the time Miguel was in middle school, he was getting increasingly tired of being tripped and shoved and having his glasses broken by "redneck jocks." Then he made a discovery. He found that yet another drug, crystal meth, made him highly aggressive and absolutely fearless. "If anyone messed with me," he remembers, "I had absolutely no qualms about beating them until I was hamburger. I felt nothing. And because they were basically cowards, they would eventually back off. On meth, I was crazy enough to scare them."

# Miguel

Even through his years of addiction, reading has always
been Miguel's passion.

As he got into high school, Miguel began finding
it easier to make friends. More kids were getting into
reading and music and coming to appreciate things
that "the weird Hispanic kid" had been into for years.
He had a brief career as part of the Skinheads Against
Racial Prejudice (SHARP), wearing combat boots

and shaving his head, but his heart wasn't really in it. "Officially we were supposed to fight racists," he said, "but I eventually had to admit I was just using it as an excuse to beat up white people."

Academically, he did "horribly," except in English classes. Finally when he was a junior, "somebody figured out that I was bored out of my mind and put me in honors classes, despite my grades. That helped some." Miguel "begged" his way into college at the University of North Texas in Denton, despite his poor transcript, and decided he would stop using drugs when he left high school.

He went off to college, and within the first week met Michelle, whose dorm room he describes as "a cathedral to psychedelic art." She also had a refrigerator full of LSD. His plans to quit drugs evaporated immediately; after two semesters he and Michelle quit college together, just ahead of being expelled, and moved to Dallas. Their mutual love of drugs deepened and expanded, and scoring and hustling become the focus of their lives.

"Michelle was a master physician manipulator," Miguel remembers. "She'd go to a doctor complaining of migraines, and start 'climbing the migraine ladder.' She'd get one medication after another and go back and say, 'No, this isn't effective; the pain is too bad.' Finally she was getting a bottle of Stadol every two weeks—Stadol, a metered 1-millimeter spray that is ten times as potent as morphine." She shared the Stadol with Miguel.

Miguel decided to try college again, this time at Texas South University in Houston. He and Michelle moved into an apartment that was surrounded by clubs, and they soon saw the potential for drug-dealing there. They sold marijuana, LSD, and over-the-counter pharmaceuticals from nearby Mexico. Across the hall was a crystal meth dealer; downstairs was the guy who sold heroin. Throughout the night and early morning hours, runners would make trips from the drug apartments to the clubs.

Miguel takes a call in his Houston apartment.

# Miguel

And Miguel was sampling the wares. "I was doing all of them," he says. "They were all right there. I figured as long as I wasn't sticking a needle in my arm, I was ok. Instead of injecting the heroin I was using the Stadol bottles to snort it. It was all very hygienic, very methodical."

Michelle, however, had begun to secretly shoot up heroin. Miguel didn't know at first; when he'd ask about the marks on her arms, she'd say they were spider bites or that her cat had scratched her. But eventually the truth came out—not only was Michelle mainlining, but she owed a lot of money to the dealer.

"We thought we would get killed" over the debt, Miguel says. "But the supplier wrote it off. She was an Hispanic woman, as are many of the dealers in Texas. It's often the moms, the *abuelas* who are the dealers. They're better at it, smarter. They're not going to flip out over some stupid macho thing and kill someone."

Michelle's shooting up led to a crisis in her relationship with Miguel. "There was lots of fighting," he recalls. Eventually Michelle left to enter rehab. In a panic, and tripping on LSD, Miguel called his mother, whom he hadn't seen in a year. "I was delirious," he recalls. "I told her, 'Please come get me. I don't want to die here.'"

His mother took him home and put him in her own bed, where he thrashed through withdrawal for three horrible days. "I had the shakes, the runs, the vomiting," he says. "She was angry; she was disappointed, but she was there for me."

When the worst was over, Miguel decided to leave Houston and return to Dallas, this time with April, a girl who was Michelle's friend. "I was gonna get the hell away from that scene," he recalls. "I was going to get a normal job and be a normal person."

He did clean up, briefly, using only "a little maintenance pot," as he describes it. "But then I met a guy," he says. "You always meet a guy, you know? And I began to snort heroin again."

And on November 3, 1997, he injected heroin for

the first time. His journal entry for that day reads:

*. . . he snapped off the tourniquet and slowly eased the needle out. Two seconds later, my breath was taken away. The rush was OK, but this slow fade, this lingering shelter of narcotic womb is the stuff dreams are made of. Sorry, Michelle, you were right. This is better than we could have ever been.*

"The feeling was indescribable," he says. "I thought nothing could never hurt me. I'd never feel lonely, never feel lousy, never feel heartbroken again."

A week later, he shot April up for the first time. "And we were off to the races," he says. The two would shoot heroin together until 2001.

Heroin addiction is a full-time job. Just maintaining the balance between feeding the addiction and withdrawal takes a huge amount of time and energy, to say nothing of finding a source, raising money for the heroin, preparing and shooting it. Miguel continued to keep a journal, noting in code the days that he shot up. In January, 1998 he shot up on ten days.

Eleven months later, in December, he was up to eighteen days a month.

"If I shot up more than three consecutive days, I got sick," he recalled. "Two days on and then a day off I was queasy, but not too sick."

But he never felt well. And there were endless unsuccessful attempts to get off the stuff. Flirtations with withdrawal became a regular part of life. Withdrawal, he discovered, was hell.

"You feel rigor mortis creeping over your body," he says. "You feel yourself dying, but you can't die. Your body is rotting from the inside out. Your skeleton is trying to work its way out of your skin. You've got the runs, you're nauseated, you're shaking, you're cold. And psychologically—that's worse yet. Your mind is screaming."

As Miguel experienced it, acute withdrawal lasts for three or four days. After that there is about a week more of severe depression and stomach-flu-like symptoms. "But it's still not over then. See, the heroin molecules closely resemble a certain sugar molecule, whose receptors lie along the spinal cord," Miguel explains. "The more you use, the less able those receptors are to distinguish between heroin and that sugar. They begin to perceive the heroin as a nutrient, something you need to live. You crave it like a hungry person craves food. You've manufactured a biological need for it. And that doesn't go away."

"Worst of all, throughout your withdrawal, you are constantly thinking, 'Just one hit. Just one hit, and I won't be sick anymore.'

"And after that, when you think, 'I did it; I'm clean!' the next thought is 'Wow, my tolerance is way down. I could get *really* high now.'"

To this day, Miguel is suffering the effects of his heroin use. "I still tire easily. My stomach is still messed up. I can't digest well, and I need to take supplements to stay healthy. If I eat a bunch of sugar, it can trigger withdrawal symptoms. I can't tolerate soft drinks or candy."

This calendar is where Miguel kept track of the days
he used heroin.

But worrying about staying healthy was still far in
Miguel's future. For now, he tunneled deeper into
addiction, frequently injecting himself with cocaine
as well as heroin. He supported himself working part-

time jobs at a bagel shop, a smoothie stand, and a camping-supply store. Standing five-foot-ten, Miguel weighed 110 emaciated pounds. "I had no semblance of normal life, activities, or relationships," he said. "Everything in my life was about drugs."

Occasionally he made a half-hearted effort to clean up. During one such period, he had cut back on his drug use and enrolled in a community college in Dallas. Sitting outdoors eating lunch one day, he looked up to see April running toward him in tears. "She did it; she finally really did it," April said.

Michelle was dead. Back in Houston, Michelle's addiction had finally destroyed her. "She'd been in and out of rehab, homeless, everything," Miguel says. "She'd burned through all her family and friends. Then two days before her twenty-seventh birthday, she asked her father to drop her off at an AA meeting.

"She had a stuffed bear, Marshall, that she took everywhere she went. But as she got out of the car she gave it to her dad and said, 'Hold on to Marshall for me.'" During a break in the meeting, she went into a bathroom stall and overdosed on heroin and Xanax. She died on the bathroom floor.

Michelle's death plunged Miguel into absolute despair. "She was a wonderful person," he recalls. "Very creative. She could make magic out of thin air. She drew, wrote, made wonderful collages. I don't know if what she and I had was love, or just desperation and manipulation. But I do know that I went to her funeral and came home and proceeded to try to kill myself as quickly as possible. I was completely consumed with guilt and self-hatred."

Unfortunately—as it seemed at the time to Miguel—his tolerance for heroin was so great at this point that he found it literally impossible to die from an overdose. On several occasions his heart stopped; he was technically dead. But he kept snapping back to life.

Miguel tried working in a comic-book store, "where I was promptly fired because it was so obvious to everyone that I was an addict." He put more

Miguel grew up loving books, music, and the arts, and his
apartment reflects his interests.

and more junk into his arm until, once again, desper-
ately sick, he called his mother. She said, "Come
home, now, or you're going to die." So at age twenty-five, he moved back into his mother's house and
stayed there for three years, occasionally working as a
freelance cameraman. He was temporarily off heroin,
but was shooting up cocaine and drinking heavily.

He began dating another girl, Joanna. "On our
first date, I realized she was an ex-heroin and crack

user. She didn't tell me, but one junkie can clock another one so fast—I just knew."

The two bonded over their love of pills, marijuana and music. They made a trip to San Antonio, where they scored some heroin together. Joanna ended up OD'ing, but they got to a hospital in time.

Two weeks later, the couple traveled to New Orleans to celebrate Miguel's twenty-eighth birthday. "At first it was fine; we were drinking and dancing and having fun. But then I scored some China white heroin." Suicidal thoughts overwhelmed him again, and he filled a huge syringe and stuck it in his arm and died. "I mean, I literally died," he says. "My heart stopped."

Miguel came to in the back of an ambulance with two EMTs working on him. He was soaking wet because Joanna had tried to revive him by dumping him in a tub of water. But even in that condition, his first thought was that he wanted to carry through with his suicide. He began to mumble to the EMTs,

# Miguel

"I reserve the right to refuse treatment . . ."

Barely had the words left his mouth when the two beefy men grabbed his arms and threw him, dripping wet, out into the New Orleans night. "I said, 'Wait, wait, let me get myself together a little!' but they were so totally not taking any of my crap. They said, 'Forget it, man; we've got people all over New Orleans who need our help and want it. You want to kill yourself, you're on your own.' And they drove away.

"So," says Miguel, "I went back to our room and did more heroin."

Back in Houston, Miguel and Joanna moved in together. For about a year, they fed each other's habits. "It was just horrible," he recalls. "I was shooting up heroin and coke. My tolerance and my self-loathing had reached astronomical levels. Joanna had begun smoking crack. My father went into rehab for crack and at that same time I tried crack for the first time. How messed up is that? I guess I wanted to get an idea what he was experiencing. I learned that crack is absolutely the worst drug on the market. I mean, I was OK with being addicted to heroin—I had earned that honestly. But to have a crack craving after one hit? That's crazy stuff."

He and Joanna broke up, and he moved into the efficiency apartment where he lives now.

And then something as ordinary as a job began to turn Miguel's life around.

He was hired as a stagehand, building sets and back-drops for local theaters and the opera. "It's my dream job," he says. "I love the theater, and I'm earning union wages and overtime. I realized that I absolutely could not get incapacitated and keep this job. I didn't care about myself, but I was running heavy machinery and I didn't want to hurt someone else.

"So in January, 2003, I shot up for the last time."

On the day before his twenty-ninth birthday, Miguel went to his first AA meeting. Knowing his weakness for getting involved with drug-abusing women, he chose his meeting with care.

# Miguel

Miguel recently celebrated a full year of sobriety.

"I live in a section of Houston that is heavily gay, and I chose a meeting there because I knew most of the people attending it would be gay or bisexual or transgendered. I knew myself by then. I can handle no distractions. If I was going to a meeting filled with cute junkie girls, I wouldn't make it. Here there were no distractions. It was the only way for me."

Last March, Miguel celebrated a year of sobriety. He reports, "It's been really great. I'm still working as a stagehand, and I work off-season back at the camping gear store. I never thought they'd take the skinny shaking junkie back, but they did." He has also started his own small videography and film editing company.

His father, he reports, "is still who he is." "He's still a remarkable human being. Right now, he's teaching videography to kids. I hear from his girlfriends that sometimes he's tolerable, and sometimes he sleeps in his van."

But he has grown to know and appreciate his mother more than ever before. "I really like what I know of her humanity and endurance. I owe her a lot."

Right now, Miguel is single—an unusual state of affairs for him. "Although I'll be thirty-two next year, I don't really feel prepared for a serious relationship," he says. "Addiction really messes up your development, and I feel like I'm about ten years behind where I ought to be.

"But I'm happier and more excited about what I'm doing that I ever thought possible. My life is

Miguel shares a laugh with a friend. After cutting drugs out of his life, he has energy to make plans for the future.

pretty good. I want everyone hearing my story to know that for sure no matter how far gone you seem to be, there is capacity for hope and survival and change."